DATE DUE			

T 10036

636.1   Frisch, Carlienne
Fri
          Horses

 GUMDROP BOOKS - Bethany, Missouri

Responsible Pet Care

Horses

Responsible Pet Care

Horses

CARLIENNE FRISCH

Rourke Publications, Inc.
Vero Beach, FL 32964

Library of Congress Cataloging-in-Publication Data

Frisch, Carlienne, 1944–
  Horses / by Carlienne A. Frisch
    p. cm. – (Responsible pet care)
  Summary: Discusses the different varieties of horses and how
they should be housed, fed, groomed, and trained.
  ISBN 0-86625-189-8
  1. Horses–Juvenile literature. [1. Horses.] I. Title. II. Series.
SF302.F75 1991
636.1–dc20   90-42161
                                                      CIP
                                                       AC

CONTENTS

Is A Horse For You?

The horse has been around for 60 million years. It was one of the first domesticated animals. It helped people travel and did much of the work that machines now do. Today, horses are used mostly for pleasure. They are pets and show horses. Seven million horses are companions for people in the United States.

Today's horses are graceful and sleek. They come from Oriental and Arabian **breeds**. Some people may also own ponies, burros, or mules as riding pets. All are members of the horse family, called *Equidae*.

Horses were once a means of transportation and labor. Today they are kept mainly for pleasure.

All horses must get regular exercise in order to stay healthy. Shown above is an Appaloosa, a breed known for its spotted coat.

Taking care of a horse usually takes a couple hours each day. A healthy horse needs exercise. If the pasture or pen is large enough, the horse can exercise itself. If not, the horse benefits from being ridden or led twice a day. Horses are healthiest and happiest in a large pasture with water, food, and shelter from the weather. They must have protection from sun, insects, and storms. Indoor housing should be large enough for the horse to be comfortable, and should have a dry, soft bed protected from the weather. The stall will need daily cleaning.

A horse should have a good genetic, or inherited, background. It must have a favorable environment, including nutritious food, regular care, and proper training.

A satisfactory riding horse can be bought for about $1,000. Care may cost up to several hundred dollars a month. Some people board their horses at a commercial stable, where the horses are cared for and exercised daily. With good care, most horses live to be about 25 years old. They become companions and friends of their owners.

Varieties of Horses

Eohippus, the "dawn horse" that lived 60 million years ago, was four hands, or 16 inches, high at the withers. Withers are the highest point of the horse's back, between the shoulder blades. A **hand** is four inches, the average width of an adult hand.

Today's riding, or light, horses are 14.5 to 16.5 hands tall. They weigh up to 1,300 pounds. They include the American Saddle Horse, Appaloosa, Lipizzan, Mustang, Quarter Horse, Thoroughbred, and many others. Any horse over 16.5 hands is a work or draft horse, such as the Belgian, Clydesdale, or Percheron. Some weigh more than 2,000 pounds. Ponies, such as the Appaloosa, Shetland, and Welsh pony, are smaller than 14.5 hands. Most weigh less than 800 pounds. The horse family also includes the American Jack, the burro or donkey, and the mule. There also are wild animals in the horse family, such as the zebra. They are not kept as pets in the United States. They can be seen in zoos.

All four legs of this chestnut Arabian are marked with socks.

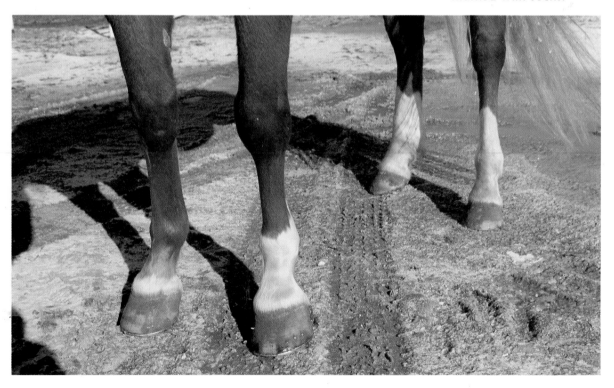

*This bay Thoroughbred
has a star on its forehead.*

Horses come in many colors. A bay horse's coat, or hair, is a mixture of red and yellow. A brown horse is almost black. A black horse is completely black. A chestnut or sorrel is reddish. A true white horse is born white and stays that way. Some horses are gray. There also are mixed colors. A dun horse is yellowish with a dark stripe down its back. Paint or pinto horses have white and colored patches. Roan horses have a colored coat with white hairs growing everywhere on it. A palomino is a gold-colored horse with a blond or silver mane and tail.

Markings are part of a horse's looks, too. Any small white mark on the forehead is called a star. White foot markings that go up the leg from the hoof are called socks, boots, or stockings.

Buying A Horse

The first step in choosing a horse is to decide why you are buying one. What will the horse's purpose be? Will it be for only one person to ride? Will it be for the whole family? Will it be ridden in horse shows?

Look for a horse with good **conformation**, or body build, and good health. A pleasant disposition, or personality, also is important. Before buying a horse, you should know the parts of the horse, how to look for body faults, and the horse's age. Ask the seller to let you try the horse before you buy it. You can have a veterinarian examine the horse for health and age. A horse's age can usually be determined by its teeth.

A horse should be the right size for its rider. A child might choose a pony, such as this Anglo-Arabian pony that has a "blaze" marking on its face.

The Quarter Horse is a muscular saddle horse. It can run very fast for distances up to a quarter of a mile.

The hindquarters, or back legs and hips, are the most important. They are the horse's source of power. The hips and thighs should be firm, with good muscles. Strong legs, well under the horse, will support its weight properly. The feet should be large enough to support the horse, but not so big that the horse stumbles. The neck needs sturdy muscles to support the head. Look for a horse with a nicely shaped head. Large, flared nostrils allow the horse to breathe easily. The eyes should be large, wide open, and clear.

A smooth back, with firm muscles, is important. A strong and firm chest, not too narrow or wide, is ideal. Watch out for a belly that pulls up. This is a sign of sickness.

The horse should be the right size for the rider. A child might choose a pony. A heavy person needs a larger horse. A tall person will want a tall animal. Choosing a healthy horse of the right size and personality will help the owner have many happy hours in the saddle.

Housing

A horse can live in either a pasture or a stable. The pasture is the horse's natural home. Your pet will need feed, water, and protection from sun, insects, and storms. The pasture must be fenced, but not with barbed wire. An electric fence may be used. Be sure there is plenty of grass. Low, swampy areas should be drained to control insects that might bite the horse. Poisonous plants, such as foxglove, ragwort, or nightshade, can kill a horse. Make sure they do not grow in the pasture.

The owner must always provide water in a clean trough or container unless there is a creek, pond, or other natural water source in the pasture. Do not use a water or feed container that is worn out or has sharp edges. Horses also can get hurt on tools, shovels, or rakes left in the pasture.

A paddock lets a horse get a little exercise and fresh air on its own.

A horse's stall should have low walls and measure at least 10 by 10 feet.

A horse that is kept in a stable needs its own stall as a separate place to feed and rest. The walls of the stall should go only half way to the ceiling, to give the animal light and air. Make each stall at least 10 by 10 feet, with a large door on the south side that opens into a **paddock** or pen. A pen at least 30 by 90 feet lets the horse get the proper exercise.

Dry, soft straw, wood shavings, or sand make a comfortable bed. It must be protected from cold winds and drafts. Each stall should have a feed rack, or box, and a supply of fresh water.

The stable must be kept clean. Mucking out, or daily cleaning, will keep the stable from smelling bad and from becoming a breeding area for insects and disease.

Feeding And Watering

Horses need two kinds of feed. They need **roughage** and grain. These must be fed in the right amounts. Too much feed causes a horse to become fat, inactive, and sick. Too little feed causes the horse to be skinny and susceptible to disease.

The best, most natural, roughage is high-quality pasture grass. Hay, or dry grass, also is good. All hay should be bright green and free from mold and dust. Mold and dust can cause horse colic.

A horse that isn't ridden can live on pasture grass alone. A horse that is ridden one to three hours a day needs 1.25 to 1.5 pounds of hay for every 100 pounds of its body weight every day. It also should be fed 0.4 to 0.75 pounds of grain per 100 pounds of weight each day. Oats, corn, and barley are usually used. A harder-working horse will need more grain and less roughage.

Fresh water, feed, a salt block, and a soft bed should be provided in a horse's stall.

A cat enjoys a sunbath in a horse stable. Cats help control rodents that might be attracted to the feed stored in a stable.

Feed your horse on a regular schedule, two or three times a day. Have a feed box for each horse. Offer hay first, in a manger or large box. Grain should be fed in a clean box that does not spill. Have a block of salt always available. A horse that works hard enough to sweat freely needs a tablespoon of salt in its grain each day. Any change in feed or ration should take place gradually over three or four days.

Offer your horse water before feeding, and again 30 minutes after a meal. Do not water your pet for at least an hour after exercise or while hot, unless it is on a trail ride. Never water a horse that has been working and then let it stand still. The horse must move on right after watering to avoid cramps and colic. Never allow a horse to exercise after a full feed, or meal.

Cleaning And Grooming

Taking care of the horse's hair coat is called grooming. Proper grooming cleans the hair, keeps the skin in good condition, and helps prevent skin diseases and **parasites**. Grooming means cleaning and brushing the hair with brushes, combs, and grooming cloths. A firm, gentle touch is needed on the horse's sensitive skin.

A horse that lives in a stable needs daily grooming. Groom a pastured horse less often to let oil build up in its coat. Oil helps protect your pet from rain. A horse should be completely groomed before it is ridden and again after it has finished its day's exercise.

A horse's hooves must be checked daily for stones.

A soft brush removes oil from the horse's coat.

Starting with the head and left side of the neck, the horse owner should groom all the way around the entire body and legs. A rubber curry comb should be rubbed firmly in circles on the horse. This massages the skin and removes mud, dead hairs, and dandruff. A brush with stiff bristles takes out dirt. A softer brush takes away oil. A cloth "stable rubber" smooths and shines the horse's coat. A damp cloth or sponge is used to clean the horse's face, below the knees, and any other sensitive areas. The mane and tail are groomed with a flat metal comb.

Each hoof must be cleaned daily with a hoof pick to get out dirt or stones. Some horse owners oil each hoof to keep them from becoming dry. Horses that are ridden on roads need a metal horseshoe on each hoof. These U-shaped "shoes" help protect the foot. They are nailed on by an expert, called a **farrier**. The hoof grows like a toenail. Every six weeks, the farrier should take off the shoes, trim the hooves, and put the shoes back on.

Handling And Exercise

A horse must have exercise to stay healthy. If its pasture or paddock is large enough, it will take its own exercise. If not, it should be taken out of its stall and ridden or led for at least 30 minutes once or twice a day. A horse that isn't exercised becomes bored, crabby, and unsafe.

The rider should understand the horse and how to use horse **tack**, or equipment. Many people take riding lessons to learn these things. They learn how to saddle and bridle the horse. They learn how to mount safely. They soon know what to expect from the horse and how to be firm with it. They also learn not to startle or surprise the horse.

A Western saddle has a high pommel (front) and cantle (back).

English saddles are flatter than Western saddles. For both types, however, it is important to place padding under the saddle to prevent chafing.

There are two types of saddles used today. The English saddle is lighter and flatter than the Western saddle. The Western saddle has a higher pommel, or front, and cantle, or back. The Western saddle is sometimes called a cowboy saddle.

Saddle pads or blankets are used under the saddle to keep it from rubbing the horse's back. They also keep sweat from the horse off the saddle.

Stirrups are attached to the saddle. They are used as footrests while the rider gets on and off the horse and while riding. They are made of metal or wood covered by leather.

The bridle fits over the horse's head. It has three parts. The headpiece holds the bridle on the horse's head. The metal bit fits into the horse's mouth. The reins are leather straps connected to the bit. The rider uses the reins to put pressure on the bit. The horse feels the pressure and does what the rider wants it to do.

19

Training

There are many ways to get help in training a horse. The 4-H Club and the Pony Club of America help their members learn about horses and how to train and ride them. Some people hire a trainer to train their horse or to help them train it. Others buy a horse that already has been trained.

Training begins with halter-breaking when the **foal** is a few weeks old. The owner puts a strong halter and rope on the foal and ties it to a strong post. The foal soon learns that the halter won't break and that it cannot run away. Then comes teaching the foal to lead, or walk along with the trainer. Pulling on the halter to the right and left will get the foal to take a step. This is best done, at first, next to the **mare**, or mother horse.

This English Pelham bridle has double reins, which give the rider more control.

A palomino Thoroughbred makes jumping look easy.

When the horse is nearly two years old, a small bit is put into its mouth for an hour at a time to get the horse used to it. Later, the owner puts a long line on the halter. This lets the horse move in a small circle. This is called longeing.

Next comes driving. The owner takes the reins and walks behind the horse. The horse learns to respond to pressure on the bit. Eventually, the horse is saddled. When the horse gets used to the feel of the saddle, the rider can mount, or sit in the saddle.

The horse will perform best for a trainer who moves slowly and speaks softly. The trainer should be calm, patient, firm, consistent, considerate, and determined. Begin with short training sessions—no more than a half-hour. As soon as the horse begins to be impatient or disinterested, end the training session. The trainer should always make sure the horse knows what is expected.

Ailments And Veterinary Care

A healthy horse is alert, attentive, and bright-eyed. Its skin is elastic and its hair coat has luster. It runs and plays for exercise and eats well. A sick horse usually won't eat and will appear listless. If it is in pain, it will be restless and will paw or scratch the ground with its front feet. The horse may sweat, lie down, try to roll over, then get up and repeat its actions.

Nearly all horses have colic at some time. This is similar to a stomachache. In horses, it is serious enough to sometimes cause death. A veterinarian should be called immediately. Lead the horse at a walk until the vet comes. Colic usually is caused by irregular feeding and watering, or by intestinal worms.

Strapping on saddles or blankets too tightly can cause sores to develop on a horse's hide.

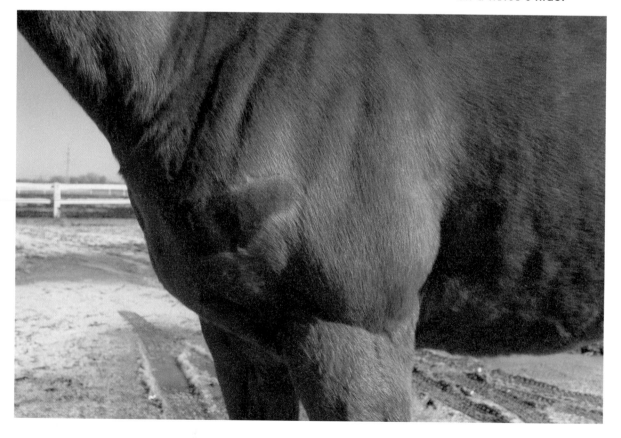

Jumping horses might need leg wraps and ankle braces to prevent injury.

Horses also may get respiratory diseases, common colds, and influenza. None of these is serious for an otherwise healthy horse. The horse can be vaccinated against such diseases as tetanus, influenza, and encephalitis (sleeping sickness). A local veterinarian can give you advice about which diseases to watch for in your part of the country.

Parasites are small creatures that live in or on the horse. Flies, mosquitos, and lice can be seen on the horse. They can be controlled by keeping the horse and its area clean. Internal parasites live in the horse's organs. There are 150 different species of parasites that can affect a horse. They include pinworms, tapeworms, and hookworms. A veterinarian can examine horse manure to tell what kinds of worms may be infecting the horse.

Breeding

Some people want to raise a horse from birth. They want a foal, or baby horse, born to their mare, or female horse. A female horse is ready to breed when she is 12 to 15 months of age. She will foal, or give birth, about a year later. Most horse owners, however, don't have their mares foal until they are three or four years old. (The word foal is used to describe both the baby horse and the birth of the baby.)

The female horse is bred with a male horse, or **stallion**. He should be at least two years old, but most owners don't breed stallions until they are three or four years old. The foal, or baby horse, is born 310 to 370 days later. People try to breed a stallion and mare so the foal is born in the spring. Most mares have one foal, but some have twins.

A horse's pedigree is a written record of its ancestors.

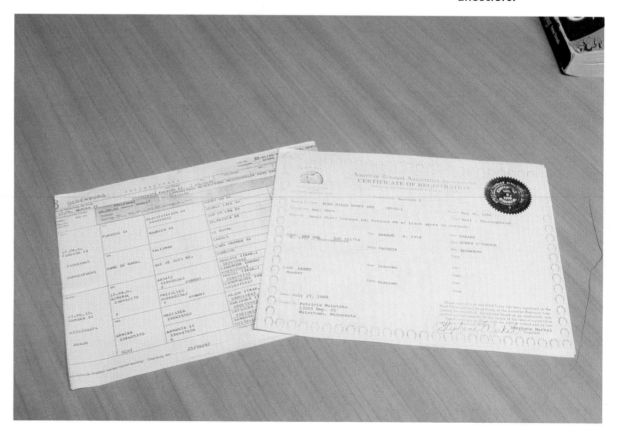

Many people breed and raise horses to show in competitions. Owners may braid their horses' manes or tails for a show.

Some mares abort, or lose, the foal before it is ready to be born. This may be caused by bacteria in the mare or by a respiratory disease. Fortunately, vaccination of the mare usually prevents this problem.

A female foal is called a **filly**. A male foal is a **colt**. Nine out of ten colts are castrated while young. They will not be used for breeding. A castrated male horse is called a **gelding**. When it grows up, it is much easier to handle and ride than a stallion.

Some people raise foals to sell them. Other people want a horse that looks a certain way. They may cross a sorrel with a white horse, for example, hoping to get a red-and-white pinto.

A horse owner who wants to raise horses to sell should get the mare's and stallion's **pedigree**, or list of ancestors. Buyers will want this information.

The Foal

Some foals are born in the pasture, others in the stable. It is best to keep a close watch on the mare near the time of the birth. She will need extra feed as foaling time approaches.

When a foal is born, it comes into the world head first. Next come the forelegs, or front legs, and then the rest of the body. Most foals weigh 90 pounds. The mare cleans the foal with her tongue. If the horse owner is there, he or she may rub the foal with clean, dry straw.

At three months old, this Oldenburg Warmblood foal has already started its training.

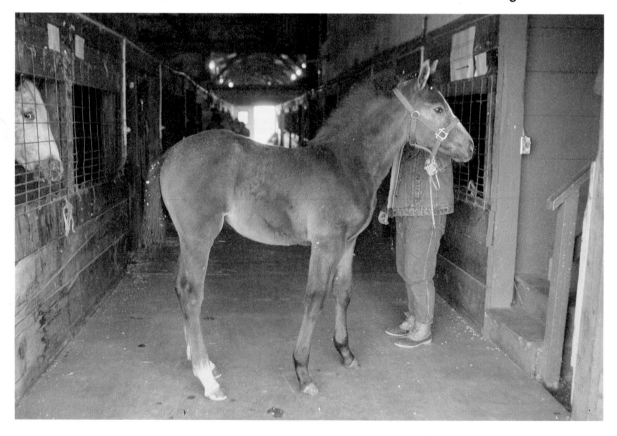

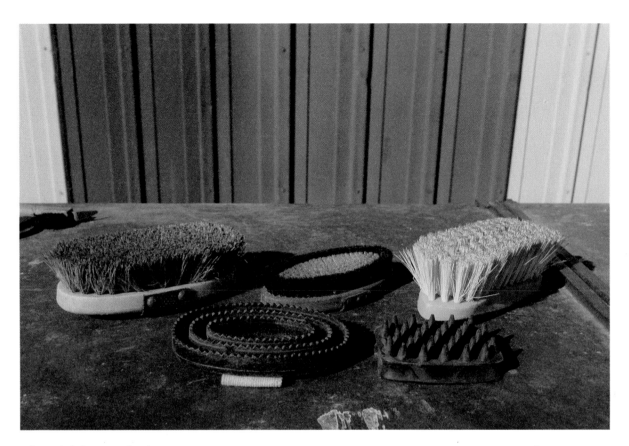

Like adult horses, foals also need to be groomed. Many types of curry combs (front) and brushes (rear) are available.

In about half an hour, the foal tries to stand up. It can stand, and even walk around, a few hours after birth. When it stands and leans against its mother, the foal learns there is milk in her **udder**. It begins to nurse, or suck milk. The milk will make it healthy and strong.

It is best to pet and handle a foal each day from the time it is born so it won't be afraid of people. The foal should be haltered and taught to lead when it is only a few weeks old.

Sometimes foals get sick. An illness called sleepers makes the foal sleepy. It won't nurse and becomes too weak to stand. With a streptococcus infection, the foal's navel, or "belly button," swells. The foal has a very high fever and diarrhea. Fortunately, most diseases a foal may get can be cured with antibiotics. It is important to pay close attention to the foal and to get medical care quickly.

Health And Longevity

People who get a horse when they are children will still have their companion and pet when they grow up. It is not unusual for a horse to live to be 25 years old. Some horses have even lived to the age of 40.

Most pleasure horses are not ridden until they are about four years old. A 10-year-old horse is considered to be in the prime of life. A horse that is given good daily care can be in top form until the age of 15. It can be ridden into its late teens.

Once a horse reaches 20, it will begin to lose weight and muscle tone. Its coat will lose its shine. The teeth and digestive system won't be as good as they used to be. The horse may not enjoy eating very much. This is the time for it to be retired to a good pasture.

Horses in good condition can be ridden into their late teens. This is a bay Thoroughbred.

Whether it wins prizes or not, a horse can make a good companion.

A retired horse still needs attention and company. It needs to be groomed. Its feet and teeth still need care. Of course, it also needs good food, fresh water, and exercise.

Although the old horse should not be ridden, the horse owner should spend time each day with the horse. The owner should talk to the horse, pet it, and take it for a walk around the pasture. A retired horse should never be fed and then ignored.

When your old horse dies, you may feel you have lost a friend. However, you will have memories of the many happy times you spent with your companion. You will remember feeding, grooming, riding, and even cleaning up after your friend.

GLOSSARY

Breeds — The different types of horses.

Colt — A young male horse.

Conformation — The bone structure, muscle, and body shape of a horse.

Farrier — A person who cares for a horse's hooves.

Filly — A young female horse.

Foal — A baby horse.

Gelding — A castrated male horse.

Hand — A unit of measure of a horse's height. One hand equals four inches.

Mare — A female horse old enough to have a foal.

Paddock — A small, enclosed area where a horse can be exercised and trained.

Parasites — Animals or plants that live on or in other animals or plants.

Pedigree — A line of ancestors, beginning with parents, then grandparents, etc.

Roughage — Grass or hay in the horse's diet.

Stallion — An adult male horse.

Tack — Horse equipment, such as the saddle.

Udder — A bag on the belly of a mammal in which milk is produced for the baby.

INDEX

Photographs by Mark E. Ahlstrom

*We would like to thank the following people
and businesses for their help in making this book:*

Heidi Haefner
Jenny Rukavina
Solyntjes Stables

Produced by Mark E. Ahlstrom
(The Bookworks)
St. Peter, MN

Typesetting and Keylining: The Final Word
Photo Research: Judith A. Ahlstrom